An Unofficial Activity Book
Amazing Activities for
Fans of Animal Crossing

Mazes, Crosswords, and Puzzles to Improve Your Skills

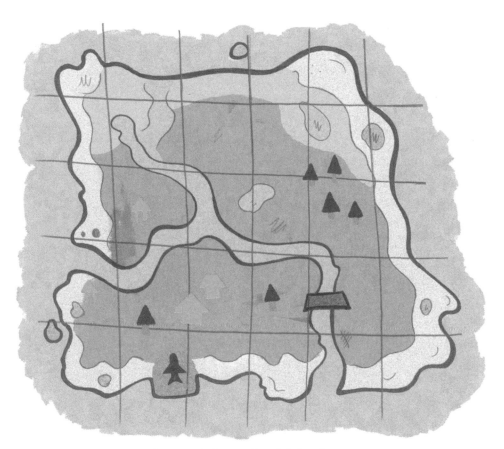

Jen Funk Weber

Sky Pony Press
New York

Sky Pony Press books may be purchased in bulk at special discounts for sales promotion, corporate gifts, fund-raising, or educational purposes. Special editions can also be created to specifications. For details, contact the Special Sales Department, Sky Pony Press, 307 West 36th Street, 11th Floor, New York, NY 10018 or info@skyhorsepublishing.com.

Sky Pony® is a registered trademark of Skyhorse Publishing, Inc.®, a Delaware corporation.

Visit our website at www.skyponypress.com.

10 9 8 7 6 5 4 3 2 1

Cover design by Brian Peterson
Cover art licensed by Shutterstock.com
Puzzles created by Jen Funk Weber
Interior art by Grace Sandford, additional
  art from Shutterstock.com.
Book design by Noora Cox

Print ISBN: 978-1-5107-6303-6

Printed in the United States of America

Table of Contents

5k Upgrade 4

Maximize Your Returns 5

Berserk Balloons 6

Crossword: Island Essential 7

The New Crew 8

Tourney Tangle 9

Talking Points 10

In Case 11

Summer Fun 12

Backstories 13

Upward Mobility 14

Nom-Nom-Nom 15

Welcome Every One 16

Crossword: Get Cracking! 17

Deal or Dud? 18

Helping Gulliver 19

Top-notch Tools 20

Color Clues 21

Dirty Tricks 22

Finders Keepers 23

Color By Number 24

Donation Agent 25

Arbor Vitals 26

Double Da Bells 27

Crossword: Evening Extravaganza ... 28

Flower Find 29

Whose House? 30

Surprise Defense 31

Fishossil? 32

Flower Fun 33

Deal or Dud? 34

Maximum Profit 35

Longevity Hack 36

Gulliver's Gifts 37

Crossword: World Changer 38

Earn Your Way 39

Missed Island Tours 40

Comparison Shopping 41

Recipe for Success 42

One Goal 43

Deal or Dud? 44

Color By Number 45

Orchard Expansion 46

Traveler's Reward 47

Bug Out 48

Crossword: Mileage Earner 49

Gone Fishin' 50

Missing Ingredient 51

Growing Goals 52

Construct a Word 53

The Ultimate Answer 54

Personality Plus 55

Answer Key 56

5k Upgrade

Begin at the tent. Can you find your way through the maze and collect 5,000 Nook Miles so you can upgrade to a house on the other side? Each leaf along the path is worth 1,000 Nook Miles.

Maximize Your Returns

Start at the ↓. Write every third letter on the spaces until all have been used. If you place them correctly, you'll learn how to get the most from your resource-gathering efforts.

C _ _ _ _ _ _ _ _ _ _ _ _

_ _ _ _ _ _ _ _ _ _ _ _

Berserk Balloons

The New Horizons balloon sender has gone berserk. You have nine balloons headed your way, but only one contains a rare seasonal DIY recipe you've been searching for. Can you follow his instructions to shoot down that one particular balloon?

1	2	3
4	5	6
7	8	9

Instructions:

1. The balloon you want is in an odd numbered square or is yellow.

2. The balloon you want is not in the bottom row, but it is above or below a red balloon.

3. The balloon you want is the same color as a balloon in the left-hand column.

GAMING TIP:
Balloons will float from one side of the island by day and the opposite side by night.

6

Crossword: Island Essential

Write answers to the clues in the boxes. Then read the highlighted columns to reveal something every player has.

Need help? Words around the edges of the page are the answers to the clues, scrambled.

PIERCE

HOTOP

SHOTCEL

NIKS

PIGNAPSN

1. _____ turtle, this large "fish," which debuts in New Horizons, can be caught in rivers at night

2. Buy these from Sable and Mabel

3. Snapshot (what you take on Harv's Island)

4. Outer layer that covers a person—or a gaming character

5. DIY _____, list of crafting ingredients

GAMING TIP: If you get lost or trapped on your island, you can call Rescue Service to pick you up for 100 Nook Miles.

What does every player have?

_____

7

The New Crew

Animal Crossing New Horizons introduced eight new special characters. Can you find the eight names and eight animal species of this new crew in the word search? They might be forward, backward, up, down, or diagonal. If you can locate them all, the remaining letters reveal a fact about your new island home.

Hint: Circle individual letters instead of whole words so it's easier to see the leftover letters.

```
T  E  P  (C) N  N  A  R  N  C
I  R  (A) E  B  M  A  A  L  Y
E  (T) V  I  E  Y  L  G  L  D
A  L  R  G  M  H  E  R  E  E
S  C  E  O  Y  A  S  N  I  M
W  L  N  P  I  D  V  D  E  E
O  D  E  O  H  M  U  N  A  S
L  N  I  G  O  A  T  J  B  R
F  I  G  D  S  L  N  U  A  O
N  S  H  E  R  B  C  T  D  H
```

AUDIE
BEAR
~~**CAT**~~
CUB
CYD
DOM
ELEPHANT
GOAT
HORSE
JUDY
MEGAN
RAYMOND
RENEIGH
SHEEP
SHERB
WOLF

___ _____ _____

___ _____ __ __ _____

Tourney Tangle

Three Fishing Tourney participants have gotten their lines tangled. Can you figure out who caught which fish?

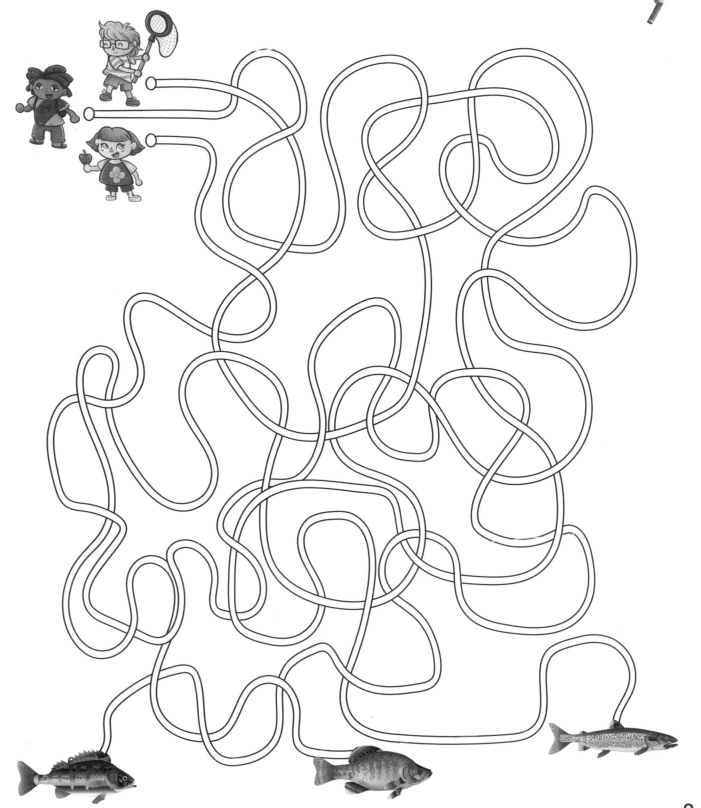

Talking Points

Pretend the green line is a mirror. Cross out letters on the top half of the grid that have incorrect letters reflected in the bottom half. Write the remaining letters from the top half on the spaces provided to discover something you can get from talking.

Z	F	T	A	G	M	L	K	T	U	J	O	S	A
B	C	R	L	E	T	Q	R	A	O	G	E	V	T
D	P	A	R	T	W	O	T	E	L	R	N	S	K

L	P	A	K	T	M	U	T	E	C	R	N	S	H
B	L	N	E	E	T	O	T	T	O	G	E	A	T
S	H	T	A	E	W	L	K	T	I	L	O	S	A

_ _ _ _ _   _ _ _   _ _ _ _ _ _

_ _ _ _   _ _ _   _ _ _ _ _ _ _ _

GAMING TIP:
To stay informed, it's a good idea to talk to *everybody* on your island.

In Case

Place the six critters in the crossword. Use the number of letters and intersecting letters to figure out where each word logically fits. The first one has been done for you. Then, transfer the numbered letters to the spaces at the bottom of the page to discover something rare.

7 Letters	8 Letters	10 Letters
CRICKET	MOSQUITO	HERMIT CRAB
~~LADYBUG~~	STINKBUG	PONDSKATER

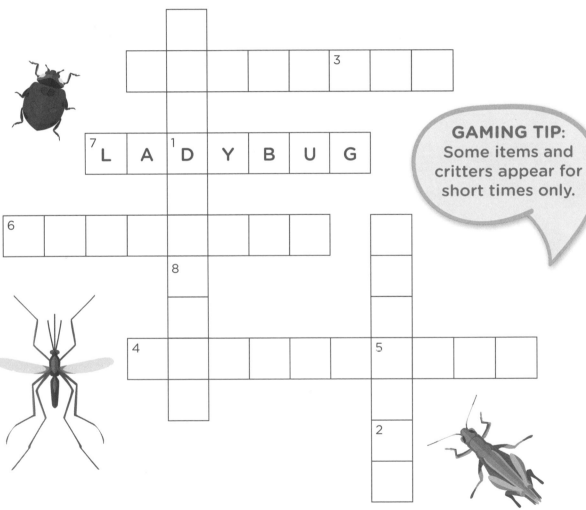

L A D Y B U G

GAMING TIP: Some items and critters appear for short times only.

One rare thing to find is a:

— — — — — —   — — — — —
5 3 5 8 1 8   6 4 2 7 7

11

Summer Fun

You're invited to this summer event with a special visitor and special swag. To find out what it is, place the six puzzle pieces that fit the shapes into the rectangle. Watch out! Pieces might be rotated or flipped, and not all pieces are used. Write the letters of the correct pieces on the spaces. If you place the pieces correctly, the name of this summer event will appear.

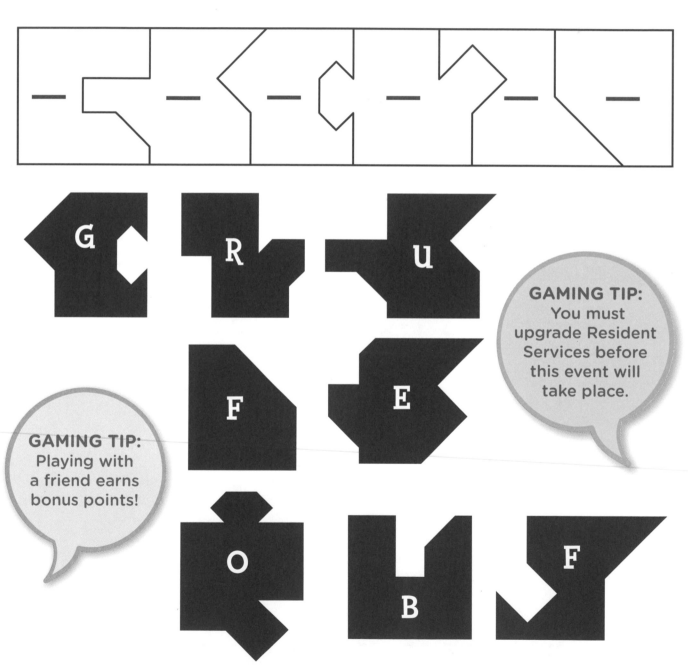

GAMING TIP: You must upgrade Resident Services before this event will take place.

GAMING TIP: Playing with a friend earns bonus points!

Backstories

Can you match each character to a tidbit from his/her backstory? Follow the maze to see if you are right. Begin at the dot below each name and follow the line downward. Every time you hit a horizontal line (one that goes across), you must take it. If you follow the lines correctly, you'll match each character to a piece of his/her past.

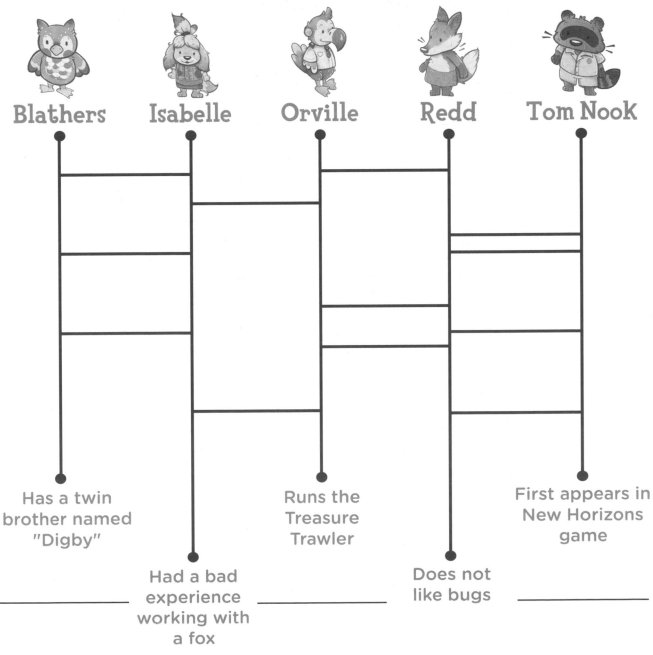

Blathers   **Isabelle**   **Orville**   **Redd**   **Tom Nook**

Has a twin brother named "Digby"

Runs the Treasure Trawler

First appears in New Horizons game

Had a bad experience working with a fox

Does not like bugs

Upward Mobility

Tom Nook will give you a recipe for a ladder, but first you have to open the Nook shop and place house plots for island residents. Choose a starting point to figure out how many house plots you need to get that super useful tool recipe.

START
here —

or
here —

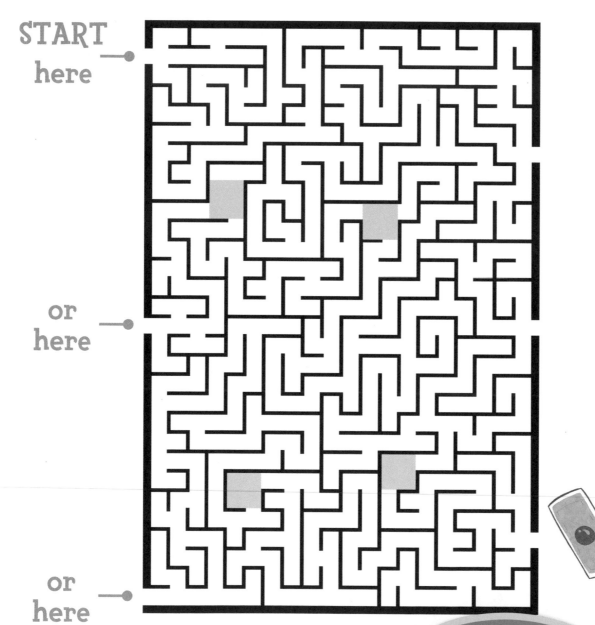

or
here —

GAMING TIP:
Until you can terraform and build inclines, you need a ladder to climb cliffs.

Nom-Nom-Nom

Start at the ↓. Write every third letter on the spaces until all have been used. If you place them correctly, you'll reveal some yummy advice.

GAMING TIP: Eating gives you strength to break rocks and dig up and pocket whole trees.

Y _ _ _   _ _ _ _ _   _ _ _ _ _

_ _ _ _ _ _ _ _ _ _ _ _ _ _

Welcome Every One

Animal Crossing New Horizons villagers have one of eight different personalities. Locate the eight personality types and the eight villager names in the word search. They might be forward, backward, up, down, or diagonal. If you find them all, the remaining letters reveal why you should welcome all personalities to your island, even grouchy ones.

Hint: Circle each letter of the words you find so you can see the leftover letters more easily.

T	Y	T	O	O	N	S	N	Y	H
P	E	D	Y	O	F	A	L	F	F
E	H	E	E	R	C	I	D	L	S
P	I	I	S	E	L	B	B	I	N
P	F	R	P	A	F	A	S	P	Y
Y	E	D	M	P	R	T	Z	S	K
J	B	R	U	C	E	E	M	Y	N
N	O	E	T	R	D	U	I	Y	A
N	R	C	L	E	G	C	X	I	R
P	E	Y	K	Y	E	O	J	S	C

CRANKY
JOCK
LAZY
NORMAL
PEPPY
SISTERLY
SMUG
SNOOTY
BRUCE
FLIP
JOEY
LILY
NIBBLES
DEIRDRE
HIPPEUX
PECAN

You should welcome all personality types to your island because

_ _ _ _ _   _ _ _ _ _ _   _ _ _ _ _ _ _ _ _ _

_ _ _   _ _ _ _ _ _ _

Crossword: Get Cracking!

Write answers to the clues in the boxes. Read the highlighted boxes to reveal a useful purchase from Nook's Cranny for customizing your island.

Need help? Words around the edges of the page are the answers to the clues, scrambled.

BARC   POSSEL

CLIFK

HOLVES

CODER

SPOUTCO

1. In your Critterpedia: Hermit _____

2. Furniture and things you put on your wall

3. Villagers Octavian and Marina are this kind of sea animal with eight legs

4. Bug artist who buys bugs for 150% their normal price

5. Another word for inclines or ramps (rhymes with *ropes*)

6. Use this to hit rocks or dig up trees

What is a good purchase if you want to customize?

_____

Deal or Dud?

Redd the fox will try to sell you a fake painting instead of the original, but don't let him trick you. Find the difference between the original painting and Redd's forged painting below and circle it. Use this skill to help you get the most out of your art purchases.

Helping Gulliver

Gulliver the seagull has washed up on your beach and needs your help. Can you find the parts to his lost communicator in this maze and bring them to him?

GAMING TIP:
Gulliver will send you a present if you help him find his communicator (cell phone) parts.

Top-notch Tools

Pretend the blue line is a mirror. Cross out letters on the top half of the grid that have incorrect letters reflected in the bottom half. Write the remaining letters from the top half on the spaces to discover an important tip about resource collection.

```
P U U Z S E A Z S T L O N E
E A S M X A E T O C K O L E
L E C U T W O S M A O D R T
─────────────────────────────
Γ E C H ⊥ W O E ⊥ Я O D E E
E ∀ K I X Γ E ⊥ O C Γ O Γ ⊥
I ∩ ⊥ W Ƨ E ∀ O Ƨ ⊥ И O ⊥
```

_ _ _   _ _   _ _ _ _ _   _ _ _   _ _

_ _   _ _ _ _ _ _ _   _ _ _ _

20

Color Clues

What determines the colors of star fragments that wash up on the beach after you wish on a shooting star? To find out, place the seven related words or phrases in the crossword. Use the number of letters and intersecting letters to figure out where each word logically fits. The first one has been done for you. Then transfer the numbered letters to the spaces at the bottom of the page. If you fill in the puzzle correctly, you'll discover how to predict and identify zodiac star colors.

4 Letters	5 Letters	7 Letters
BULL	ARIES	SCORPIO
CRAB	TWINS	SEA GOAT
~~FISH~~		

Star fragments will match the month's

Dirty Tricks

Achieve this in Animal Crossing New Horizons and earn 300 Nook Miles. Find the seven puzzle pieces that fit the shapes in the rectangle. Watch out! Pieces might be rotated or flipped, and not all pieces are used. Write the letters of the correct pieces on the spaces.

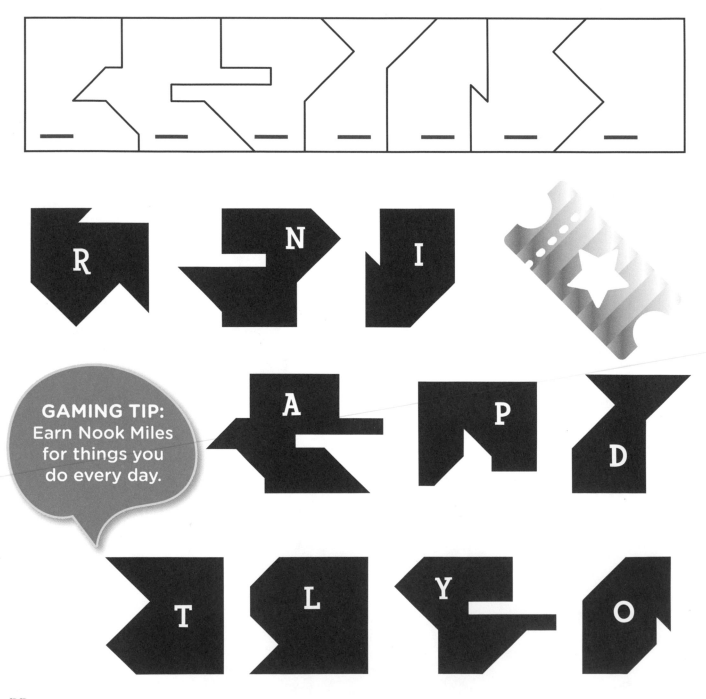

GAMING TIP: Earn Nook Miles for things you do every day.

Finders Keepers

Follow the ladder maze to see which objects promise which resources and rewards. Begin at the dot below each object and follow the line downward. Every time you hit a horizontal line (one that goes across), you must take it. If you follow the lines correctly, you'll match each object to something it might provide. Finders keepers!

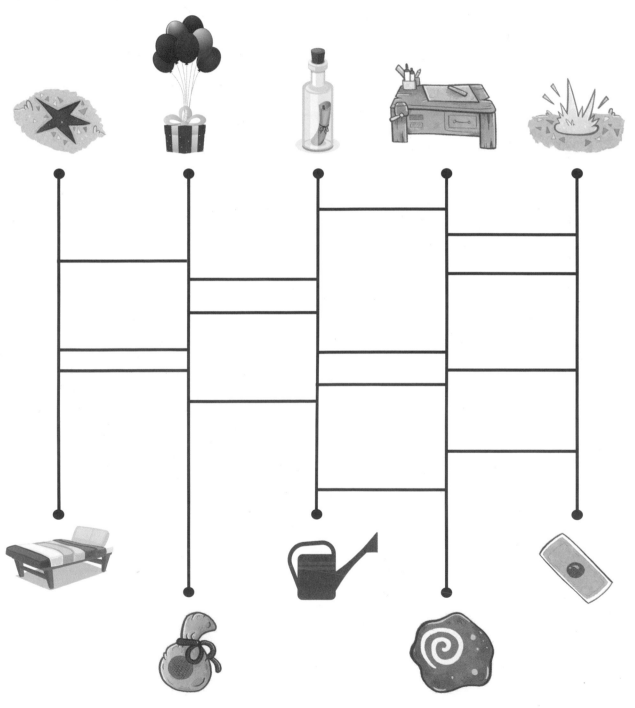

Color By Number

Color the picture to reveal the item that falls out of the star-shaped pinata you can hit on your avatar's birthday.

1 RED   **3** BROWN   **5** YELLOW

2 PINK   **4** ORANGE   **6** GREEN

Donation Agent

The museum won't be open on your island until you complete a simple task. Collect five different bugs as you go through the maze and donate them to Tom Nook at the end so you can open your island's museum.

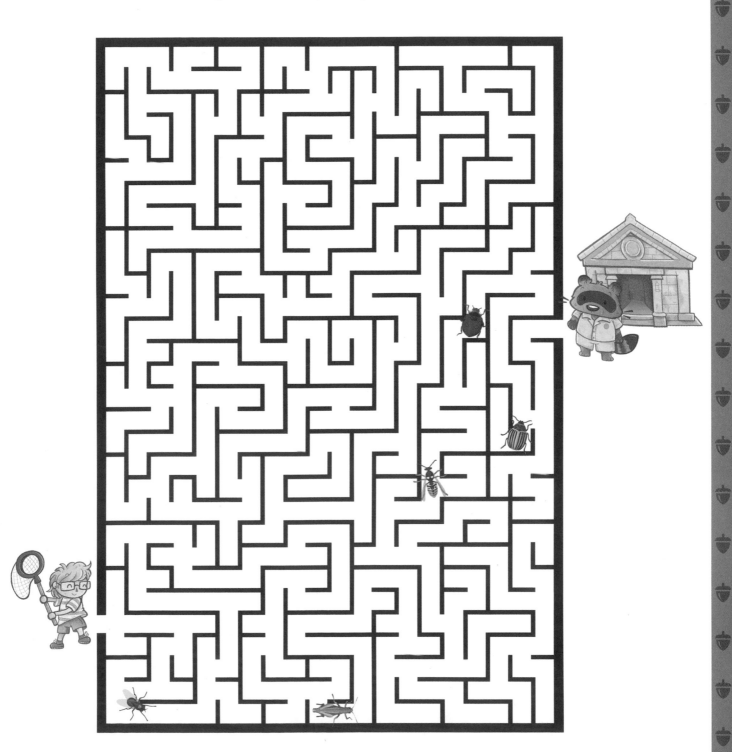

Arbor Vitals

Start at the ↓. Write every third letter on the spaces until all have been used. If you place them correctly, you'll reveal something all trees must have.

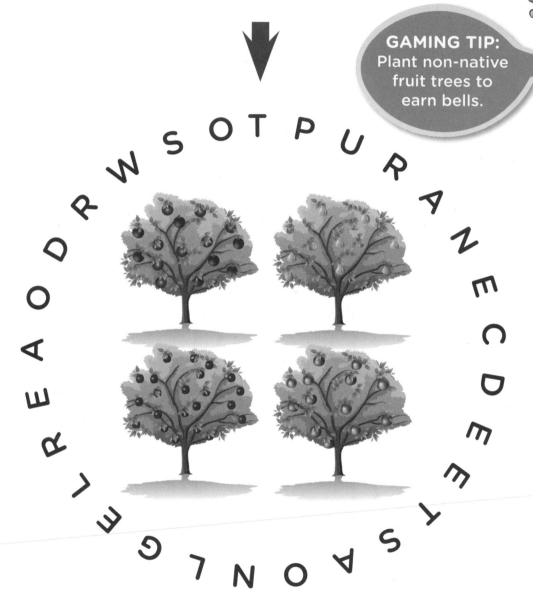

T _ _ _ _   _ _ _ _   _ _ _ _ _

_ _ _   _ _ _ _ _ _   _ _   _ _ _ _

Double Da Bells

Timmy's paying double for today's Hot Item, but you have to figure out what that item is. Can you follow the clues and earn twice as many bells for this item today?

Clues:

1. Today's Hot Item is in the middle row or a corner square.

2. Today's Hot Item requires iron nuggets to craft and is not used to catch or hold anything.

3. Today's Hot Item is not used in the garden and is not in the right-hand column.

GAMING TIP:
Hot items change daily, but when you make them you can sell them for twice as many bells as usual!

Crossword: Evening Extravaganza

Sometimes things are more than they seem. Write answers to the clues in the boxes. Read the highlighted boxes (from bottom to top) to reveal a special evening event worth seeing.

Need help? Words around the edges are the answers to the clues, scrambled.

RADOB   DELERE   STIRES

RATS

DORCER

HHAAMMII

NOWT

1. Fragments of this wash up on the beach.
2. Bulletin _____, a place to post or read messages
3. After the fish took the lure you _____ it in
4. Smaller than a city, bigger than a village
5. Set a _____, have the biggest or the most
6. Very large fish caught from the pier, worth 12,000 bells (a fish so nice they named it twice!)
7. Sable to Mable, or Celeste to Blathers

The special evening event is:

_____

28

Flower Find

Flowers make your island look nice and can increase your rating, but they're useful in another way, too. Find out how by locating the nine flowers in the word search. They might be forward, backward, up, down, or diagonal. If you can pick them all out, the remaining letters reveal something you can do with the flowers you grow.

Hint: Circle individual letters instead of whole words so it's easier to see the leftover letters. The first one's been done for you.

C	O	G	C	O	S	M	O	S	H
L	L	E	O	C	T	B	U	T	G
R	E	W	O	L	F	D	N	I	W
M	T	S	L	A	D	I	N	P	D
U	S	U	R	I	C	R	N	A	A
M	I	O	L	A	L	L	O	N	S
F	S	R	Y	I	O	Y	M	S	B
E	L	H	O	O	P	M	S	Y	E

COSMOS
GOLD ROSE
HYACINTH
LILY
MUM
PANSY
ROSE
TULIP
WINDFLOWER

GAMING TIP:
Hyacinths, mums, and windflowers are new to Animal Crossing New Horizons.

_ _ _ _ _ _ _ _ _   _ _ _ _   _ _ _

_ _ _ _ _ _ _   _ _ _ _   _ _ _ _ _ _

Whose House?

Three friends are fishing and catching critters together on this island, but only one lives here. It's the one who has a house. Follow the maze to determine which player lives on this island: Zipster, Stella, or Rook.

Zipster

Stella

Rook

GAMING TIP:
You can have up to 8 people living on your island.

Surprise Defense

Pretend the orange line is a mirror. Cross out letters on the top half of the grid that have incorrect letters reflected in the bottom half. Write the remaining letters from the top half on the spaces to discover a surprising method you can use to defend yourself in a dangerous situation.

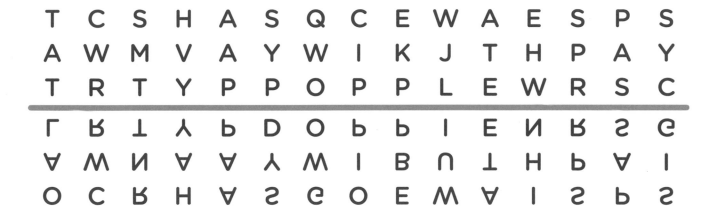

```
T  C  S  H  A  S  Q  C  E  W  A  E  S  P  S
A  W  M  V  A  Y  W  I  K  J  T  H  P  A  Y
T  R  T  Y  P  P  O  P  P  L  E  W  R  S  C
─────────────────────────────────────────────
L  R  T  Y  P  D  O  P  P  I  E  N  R  S  C
A  W  N  A  Y  I  W  I  B  U  T  H  P  A  T
O  C  R  H  A  S  C  O  E  M  W  I  S  P  S
```

_ _ _ _ _   _ _ _ _ _   _ _ _ _ _   _ _ _ _

_ _ _ _ _   _ _ _ _ _ _ _

Fishossil?

It's been around since the time of dinosaurs, but it's not a fossil. What is it? To find out, place the six critters in the crossword. Use the number of letters and intersecting letters to figure out where each word logically fits. One letter has been done for you. Transfer the numbered letters to the spaces with the same numbers. If you fill in the puzzle correctly, you'll find something very cool, and very rare.

6 Letters	7 Letters	8 Letters
DORADO	PIRANHA	CRAWFISH
SALMON	TADPOLE	STURGEON

GAMING TIP: You can find this all year, but only in rain or snow.

This ancient creature is called a:

___ ___ ___ ___ ___ ___ ___ ___ ___ ___ ___
8   3   5   2   6   8   6   1   4   7

32

Flower Fun

To find out what you can create by combining flowers, place the seven puzzle pieces that fit the shapes into the rectangle. Watch out! Pieces might be rotated or flipped, and not all pieces are used. Write the letters of the correct pieces on the spaces. If you place the pieces correctly, you'll spell out your challenge.

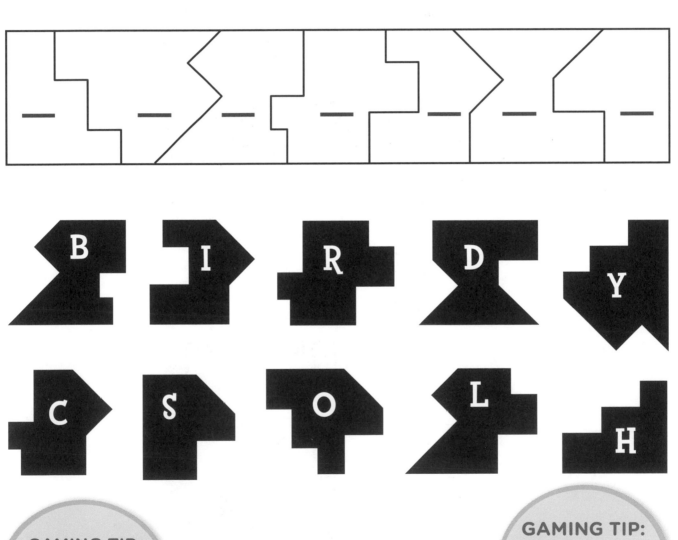

GAMING TIP: You can buy flower seeds from Nook's Cranny.

GAMING TIP: Watered flowers sparkle.

33

Deal or Dud?

Redd the fox will try to sell you a fake painting instead of the original, but don't let him trick you. Find the difference between the original painting and Redd's forged painting below and circle it. Use this skill to help you get the most out of your art purchases.

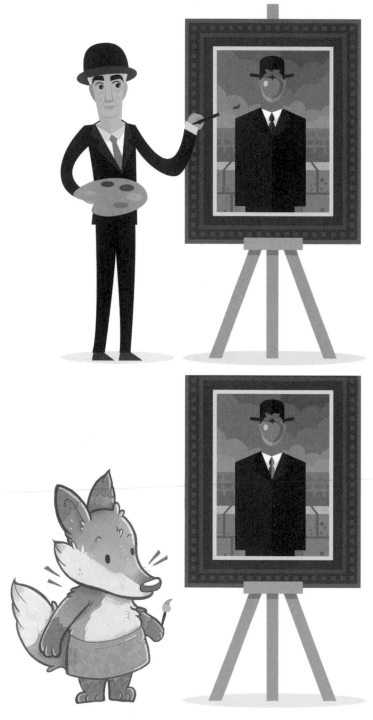

Maximum Profit

You're out collecting items and find something you want to sell. Complete the maze to discover what you found and who you should sell it to.

GAMING TIP:
Flick pays 1.5 times the Nook's Cranny price for bugs, and C. J. pays 1.5 times the price for fish.

START

Flick

C. J.

Timmy and Tommy

Longevity Hack

Start at the ↓. Write every third letter on the spaces until all have been used. If you place them correctly, you'll reveal a tip for extending the life of your tools.

C _ _ _ _ _ _ _ _ _   _ _ _   _ _ _   _ _ _ _ _   _ _ _   _ _ _

_ _ _   _ _ _ _ _ _ _ _   _ _ _   _ _ _ _

36

Gulliver's Gifts

Gulliver the seagull has washed up on your shore again. Help him find the names of ten souvenirs in the word search. They might be forward, backward, up, down, or diagonal. If you can locate them all, the remaining letters will spell something else you might get if you help Gulliver often enough.

Hint: Circle individual letters instead of whole words so it's easier to see the leftover letters.

```
N  A  B  R  U  T  G  P  E  S
E  U  T  A  T  S  I  A  O  M
L  T  T  A  N  G  I  U  F  L
D  P  T  C  T  Y  T  G  L  S
E  O  Y  A  R  H  L  O  D  P
R  S  I  R  P  A  D  H  A  H
M  L  O  O  A  A  C  G  V  I
A  E  L  L  L  M  O  K  D  N
S  E  I  U  Y  D  I  R  E  X
K  E  H  C  A  I  P  D  E  R
```

~~ELDER MASK~~
HULA DOLL
MOAI STATUE
NUTCRACKER
PAGODA
PIGTAIL
PYRAMID
SOUTH POLE
SPHINX
TURBAN

If you help Gulliver enough, you might

___ _ _____ ____ _____

___ _____

Crossword: World Changer

Write answers to the clues in the boxes. Read the highlighted boxes to reveal what is arguably the quintessential achievement in Animal Crossing New Horizons.

Need help? Words around the edges are the answers to the clues, scrambled.

DURBIE · · · THING · · · DESES · · · WERDEE

PLEAPS · · ANIMAL

GRIBED · · WINDGED

1. _____ treasure, for which you'll need your shovel
2. They can become flowers and trees
3. 🍎🍎🍎🍎
4. The clam that makes fish bait
5. When Celeste, the owl, is likely to visit
6. "_____ Season," the month of June
7. "Greedy _____," a Nook Miles+ achievement for selling unwanted greenery
8. If you have this, you don't need your vaulting pole

The achievement is: _____

Earn Your Way

Can you match each Nook Miles Achievement to its task? Follow the maze to see if you are right. Begin at the dot below each achievement and follow the line downward. Every time you hit a horizontal line (one that goes across), you must take it. If you follow the lines correctly, you'll know what you have to do to earn those Nook Miles.

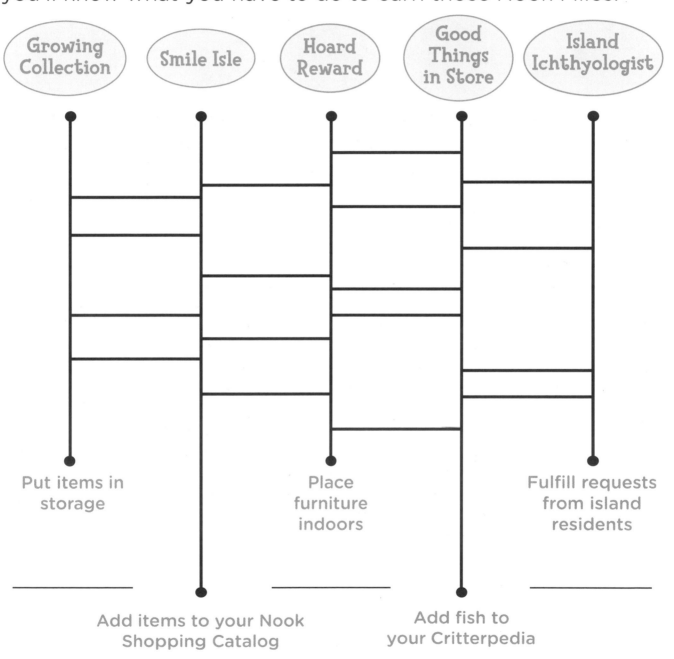

Growing Collection

Smile Isle

Hoard Reward

Good Things in Store

Island Ichthyologist

Put items in storage

Place furniture indoors

Fulfill requests from island residents

Add items to your Nook Shopping Catalog

Add fish to your Critterpedia

Missed Island Tours

You've purchased a Mystery Island Tour, and you can't wait to see which island you'll land on! Follow the maze to find out.

Comparison Shopping

Pretend the green line is a mirror. Cross out letters on the top half of the grid that have incorrect letters reflected in the bottom half. Write the remaining letters from the top half on the spaces to discover a reason to comparison shop.

```
T E S E R L L L Y O H U R T U G A
Z R N I V P S O P F N N O T J C H
K O K E R L M I S C L A W N S D S
─────────────────────────────────
H E R E R T H I S E A R N E D S
S R N I A P S O R E N H O T I C H
I T S E P L R L Y O I N R T N C E
```

_ _ _ _ _   _ _ _ _   _ _ _ _ _ _ _

_ _   _ _ _ _   _ _ _ _ _ _ _

GAMING TIP:
Smart gamers wait patiently for the value of their items to go up before they sell them!

Recipe for Success

Place the seven tool-related words or phrases in the crossword. Use the number of letters and intersecting letters to figure out where each word logically fits. Transfer the numbered letters to the spaces at the bottom of the page. If you fill in the puzzle correctly, you'll discover a recipe you need for success in New Horizons.

AXE
NET
SHOVEL
UPGRADE
DURABILITY
FISHING ROD
WATERING CAN

A recipe for New Horizons success:

___ ___ ___ ___ ___ ___   ___ ___ ___ ___   ___ ___ ___ ___ ___
10   5   2   8   8   7   6   9   9   1   8   9   9   4   3

One Goal

Whether you're just starting to play Animal Crossing New Horizons or have put in 300 hours, the goal is the same. To name that goal, identify the seven puzzle pieces that fit the shapes in the rectangle. Watch out! Pieces might be rotated or flipped. Write the letters of the correct pieces on the spaces. Not all pieces are used.

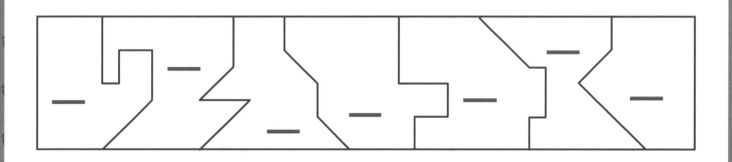

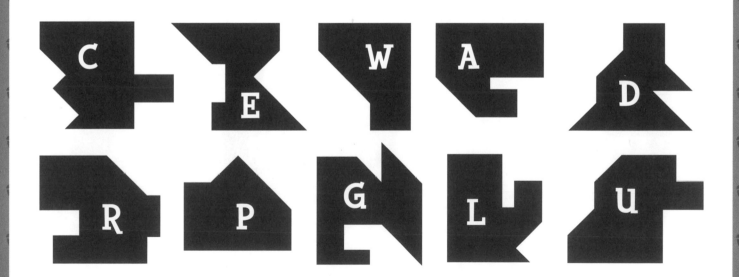

Every player's goal is to:

__ __ __ __ __ __ __

Deal or Dud?

Redd the fox will try to sell you a fake painting instead of the original, but don't let him trick you. Find the difference between the original painting and Redd's forged painting below and circle it. Use this skill to help you get the most out of your art purchases.

Color By Number

Color the picture to reveal something that Kicks the skunk sells in New Horizons.

1 RED **3** BROWN **5** DARK BLUE

2 YELLOW **4** LIGHT BLUE **6** GREEN

Orchard Expansion

Animal Crossing New Horizons player, Farmer in the Bells, is looking to expand his native cherry orchard with non-native fruits. Follow the maze to discover what fruit he's able to bring back from a friend's island today: pears, apples, or oranges.

GAMING TIP:
Letters from Mom can be a source of non-native fruit. If you receive some, plant them!

Traveler's Reward

Start at the ↓. Write every third letter on the spaces until all have been used. If you place them correctly, you'll reveal a good reason to get off your island and explore.

GAMING TIP: All Mystery Islands have a workbench in case one of your tools breaks while you're exploring.

F I N D   C O C O N U T S   O N

M Y S T E R Y   I S L A N D   T O U R S

Bug Out

You see nine bugs, but you only have time to catch one—and you left your Critterpedia at home. Follow the clues to figure out which bug you need for your collection.

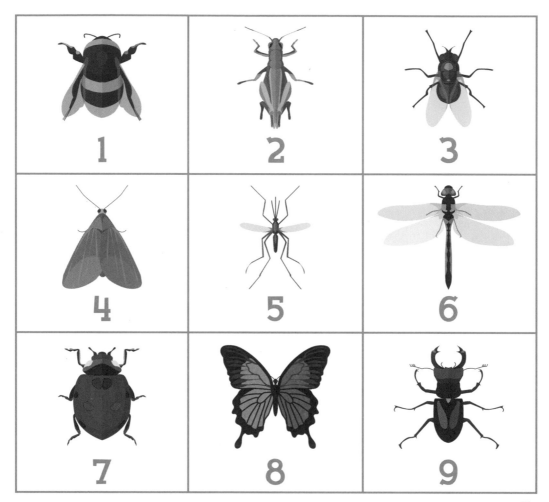

Clues:

1. The bug you need is in the bottom row, the right-hand column, or the center square. (But it's not the fly.)

2. The bug you need is in an odd-numbered square or a square with a number less than 4. (But it's not the beetle in square 9.)

3. The bug you need is found on flowers during the day.

Crossword: Mileage Earner

Write answers to the clues in the boxes. Read the highlighted boxes to reveal a Nook Miles+ achievement that can lead to crafting, more collecting, and more bells!

Need help? Words around the edges are the answers to the clues, scrambled.

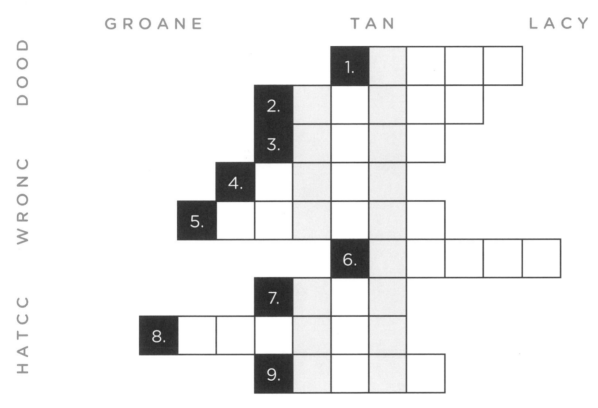

1. Resource found in rocks
2. A wreath worn on your head
3. "_____ of the Valley," grows on 10-star islands
4. Part of a skeleton found as a fossil (not the skull)
5. Sometimes a woman in distress, or a fly
6. What you try to do with fish and bugs—or a baseball
7. A critter found on rotten turnips
8. Citrus fruit tree
9. Orville's species

The achievement is called: _____

Gone Fishin'

Find the eleven fish in the word search. They might be forward, backward, up, down, or diagonal. When you catch them all, write the remaining letters in order from top to bottom and left to right on the spaces to reveal a secret about these particular fish.

Hint: Circle individual letters instead of whole words so it's easier to see the leftover letters.

ARAPAIMA   BLUE MARLIN   GOLDEN TROUT   SAW SHARK
AROWANA   COELACANTH   GREAT WHITE SHARK   STRINGFISH
BARRELEYE   DORADO   NAPOLEONFISH   STURGEON

```
                K  H  T
                R  H  S
                A  E  S  I  E
          A  H  R  E  T  F  H  E  M                          E  O
       S  S  S  T  R  I  N  G  F  I  S  H              T  D  Y  V
    A  W  L  U  A  B  N  O  E  G  R  U  T  S           O  L  E
 E  A  F  K  R  A  H  S  E  T  I  H  W  T  A  E  R  G  I  L  S
 H  S  T  H  T  N  A  C  A  L  E  O  C  H  E  Y  A  R  E  A  E
 G  O  L  D  E  N  T  R  O  U  T  L  L  W  D  O  R  T  H  R  T
 E  N  T  H  A  R  A  P  A  I  M  A  O  O           U  S  R
    A  N  N  I  L  R  A  M  E  U  L  B           D  B  A  E
    A  R  O  W  A  N  A  L  L                       B  S
    A  N  D  U  P
```

_ _ _ _ _   _ _   _ _   _ _ _ _

_ _ _ _ _ _ _ _   _ _ _ _ .   _ _ _ _ _ ' _ _

_ _ _   _ _ _ _ _ _   _ _ _   _ _ _ _ _ _ _ _

_ _ _ _ _   _ _ _   _ _ .

Missing Ingredient

You only have the ingredients to make one of these DIY recipes. To find out which ingredients you have, start at the recipe cards and make your way out of the maze.

Bamboo Speaker

Shell Fountain

Tulip Surprise Box

5 x Giant Clam
3 x Stone

5 x Red Tulip
3 x Softwood

3 x Bamboo
1 x Iron Nugget

GAMING TIP:
You'll earn more selling crafted items than selling raw materials.

Growing Goals

Pretend the green line is a mirror. Cross out letters on the top half of the grid that have incorrect letters reflected in the bottom half. Write the remaining letters from the top half on the spaces to discover a way to expand your growing options.

```
Y  S  P  O  U  C  A  L  R  N  P  L  A  W  N  Z  T
K  C  O  C  Q  M  O  N  U  L  I  T  T  R  E  F  E
S  O  N  S  P  A  N  S  D  V  P  D  A  T  H  S  N
─────────────────────────────────────────────────
S  O  N  S  B  A  N  E  D  A  P  C  A  T  H  S  N
T  C  O  C  O  N  U  N  T  H  T  R  E  E  E
Y  N  O  O  N  C  A  T  L  N  P  L  A  U  N  Z  T
```

___ ___ ____ ____ _____

_____ __ ___ _____

Construct a Word

Construct a word on the spaces by placing the nine building words in the crossword. Use the number of letters and intersecting letters to figure out where each word logically fits. One letter has been given to help you. Transfer the numbered letters to the spaces at the bottom of the page. If you fill in the puzzle correctly, you'll construct a word that will allow you to build the island of your dreams.

4 Letters	5 Letters	6 Letters
DIRT	CLIFF	CUSTOM
PATH	GRASS	DESIGN
RAMP	WATER	PERMIT

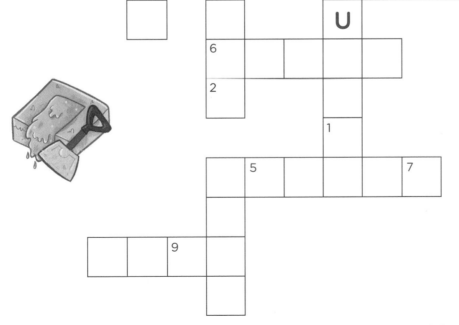

The word you constructed is

$\overline{7}$ $\overline{5}$ $\overline{9}$ $\overline{9}$ $\overline{3}$ $\overline{10}$ $\overline{1}$ $\overline{9}$ $\overline{8}$ $\overline{4}$ $\overline{2}$ $\overline{6}$

The Ultimate Answer

When someone asks, "Do you play New Horizons?" or "Do you like New Horizons?" this is the ultimate answer. To find out what it is, identify the six puzzle pieces that fit the shapes in the rectangle. Watch out! Pieces might be rotated or flipped, and not all pieces are used. Write the letters of the correct pieces on the spaces.

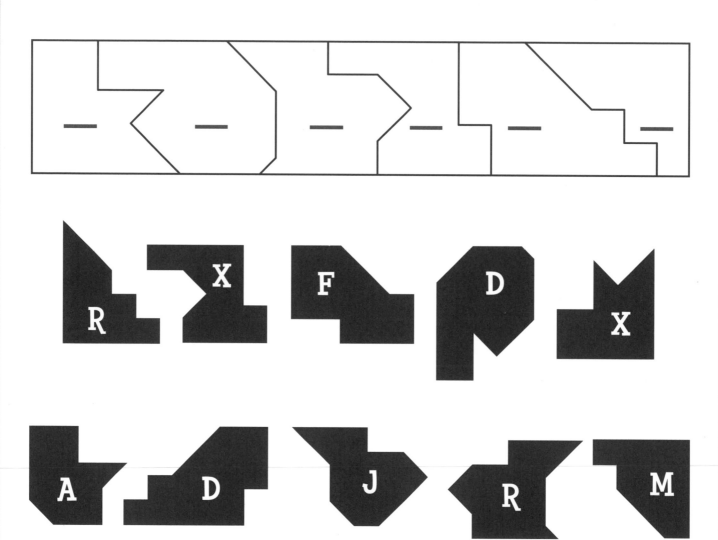

But wait—there's an extra step to cracking this code. Write the letter that comes AFTER each letter in the alphabet to truly solve the puzzle.

Personality Plus

Match each character's name to his/her personality type and his/her catchphrase. The ladders will help you out. Begin at the dot below each name and follow the trail downward. Every time you hit a horizontal trail (one that goes across), you must take it. Write the personality and catchphrase next to each character's name in the chart.

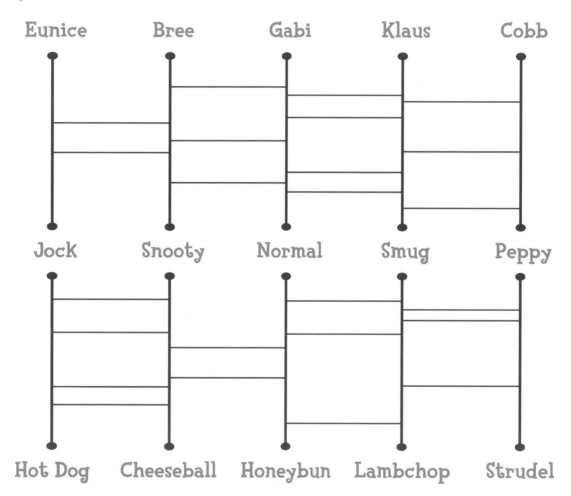

Eunice   Bree   Gabi   Klaus   Cobb

Jock   Snooty   Normal   Smug   Peppy

Hot Dog   Cheeseball   Honeybun   Lambchop   Strudel

NAME	PERSONALITY	CATCHPHRASE
Eunice		
Bree		
Gabi		
Klaus		
Cobb		

ANSWER KEY

5K UPGRADE (Page 4)

MAXIMIZE YOUR RETURNS (Page 5)

CLEAR OBJECTS NEAR ROCKS AND TREES

If there are weeds, flowers, branches, furniture, etc. around your trees when you shake them or around your rocks when you hit them, the resources you release can bounce away or disappear.

BERSERK BALLOONS (Page 6)

The green balloon in the top right corner is the balloon with your special seasonal DIY recipe.

CROSSWORD: ISLAND ESSENTIAL (Page 7)

1. SNAPPING
2. CLOTHES
3. PHOTO
4. SKIN
5. RECIPE

Every player has a NOOK PHONE.

THE NEW CREW (Page 8)

TEN ANIMAL VILLAGERS CAN LIVE ON AN ISLAND

TOURNEY TANGLE (Page 9)

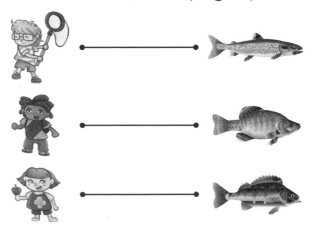

TALKING POINTS (Page 10)

TALK TO SABLE TO GET PATTERNS

IN CASE (Page 11)

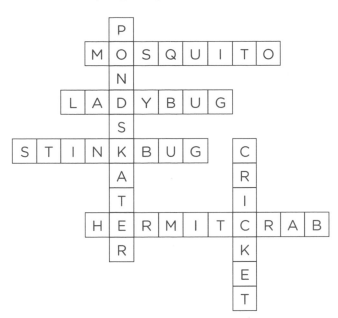

One rare thing to find is a:

CICADA SHELL

SUMMER FUN (Page 12)

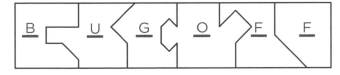

BUG OFF

Flick's Bug Off is like the Fishing Tourney: get points for catching as many bugs as you can in 3 minutes, then trade your points for special bug swag.

BACKSTORIES (Page 13)

BLATHERS — Does not like bugs

ISABELLE — Has a twin brother named "Digby"

ORVILLE — First appears in New Horizons game

REDD — Runs the Treasure Trawler

TOM NOOK — Had a bad experience working with a fox

UPWARD MOBILITY (Page 14)

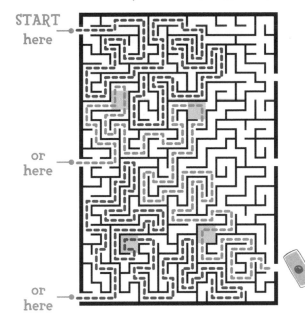

You need to place three house plots to get the ladder recipe.

NOM-NOM-NOM (Page 15)

YOU CAN EAT BAMBOO SHOOTS LIKE FRUITS

WELCOME EVERY ONE (Page 16)

You should welcome all personality types to your island because THEY OFFER DIFFERENT DIY RECIPES.

CROSSWORD: GET CRACKING! (Page 17)

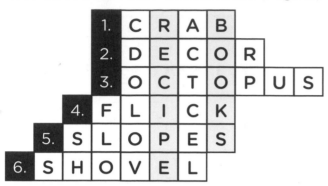

1. C R A B
2. D E C O R
3. O C T O P U S
4. F L I C K
5. S L O P E S
6. S H O V E L

RECIPE BOOKS are a good purchase if you want to customize.

DEAL OR DUD? (Page 18)

HELPING GULLIVER (Page 19)

TOP-NOTCH TOOLS (Page 20)

USE A STONE AXE TO COLLECT WOOD

If you collect wood with an iron axe, on the other hand, you'll chop the whole tree down. *Whoopsie!*

COLOR CLUES (Page 21)

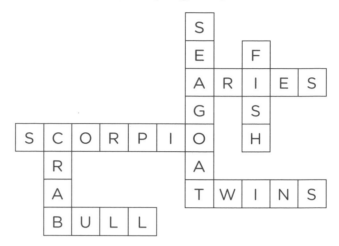

Star fragments will match the month's BIRTHSTONE COLOR.

DIRTY TRICKS (Page 22)

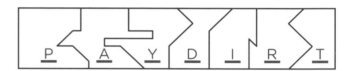

PAYDIRT

The Paydirt achievement rewards you with 300 miles for digging up a shiny spot where hidden treasure (a bag of bells) is buried. In real life, "paydirt" is what prospectors called gold.

FINDERS KEEPERS (Page 23)

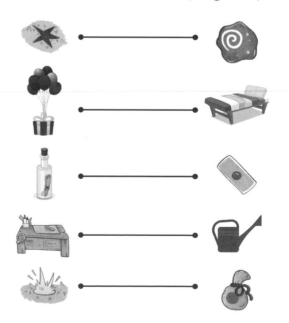

COLOR BY NUMBER (Page 24)

DONATION AGENT (Page 25)

ARBOR VITALS (Page 26)

TREES NEED SPACE ALL
AROUND TO GROW

Trees must have one free space on
all sides to grow. Be sure to plant in
open areas.

DOUBLE DA BELLS (Page 27)

DOUBLE DA BELLS (continued)

Today's Hot Item is an acoustic guitar.

CROSSWORD: EVENING EXTRAVAGANZA (Page 28)

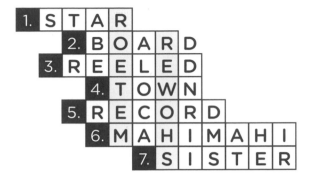

1. STAR
2. BOARD
3. REELED
4. TOWN
5. RECORD
6. MAHIMAHI
7. SISTER

The special evening event is:
METEOR SHOWER. See what
we did there? We wrote "meteor
shower" upward to make you look up—
like you have to do to see meteors!

FLOWER FIND (Page 29)

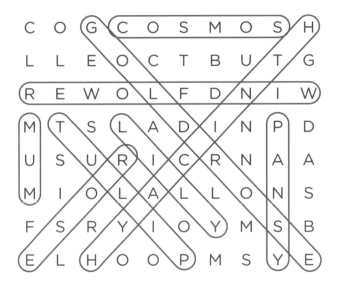

COLLECT BUGS AND SNAILS
FROM BLOOMS

Grow flowers before a Bug Off to have
more bugs available to catch.

WHOSE HOUSE? (Page 30)

It's Stella's house and island. Zipster and Rook are visiting.

SURPRISE DEFENSE (Page 31)

CHASE WASPS AWAY WITH PARTY POPPERS

When a wasp nest falls out of a tree, try popping a party popper instead of using your net. And save the nest to use in crafting.

FISHOSSIL? (Page 32)

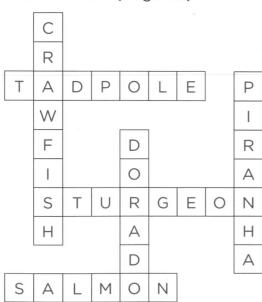

FISHOSSIL? (continued)

The creature is a real fish called a COELACANTH (Pronounced: SEEL-uh-kanth). Scientists consider it a "living fossil."

FLOWER FUN (Page 33)

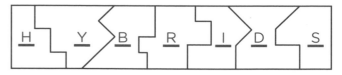

HYBRIDS

Breed flowers to get differently colored offspring. Having friends from other islands water your flowers increases the chance they'll produce offspring.

DEAL OR DUD? (Page 34)

MAXIMUM PROFIT (Page 35)

You found a bug. You should sell it to Flick to make the most profit.

LONGEVITY HACK (Page 36)

CUSTOMIZE OLD TOOLS TO RESET DURABILITY

Unfortunately, this doesn't work on axes.

GULLIVER'S GIFTS (Page 37)

```
N A B R U T G P E S
E U T A T S I A O M
L T T A N G I U F L
D P T C T Y T G L S
E O Y A R H L O D P
R S I R P A D H A H
M L O O A A C G V I
A E L L M O K D N
S E I U Y D I R E X
K E H C A I P D E R
```

If you help Gulliver enough, you might GET A NIFTY GOLD SHOVEL DIY RECIPE.

CROSSWORD: WORLD CHANGER (Page 38)

1. BURIED
2. SEEDS
3. APPLES
4. MANILA
5. NIGHT
6. WEDDING
7. WEEDER
8. BRIDGE

The achievement is: ISLAND DESIGNER.

EARN YOUR WAY (Page 39)

GROWING COLLECTION - Add items to your Nook Shopping Catalog

SMILE ISLE - Fulfill requests from island residents

HOARD REWARD - Place furniture indoors

GOOD THINGS IN STORE - Put items in storage

ISLAND ICHTHYOLOGIST - Add fish to your Critterpedia

MISSED ISLAND TOURS (Page 40)

COMPARISON SHOPPING (Page 41)

SELL YOUR TURNIPS ON OTHER ISLANDS

Ask your friends what turnips are selling for on their islands, and be sure to alert them when prices are high on your island.

RECIPE FOR SUCCESS (Page 42)

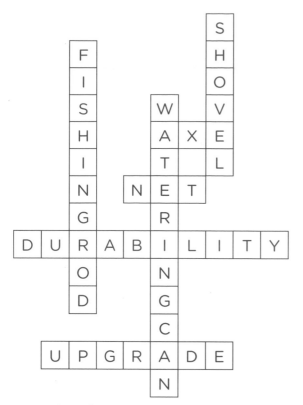

A recipe for success in New Horizons: PRETTY GOOD TOOLS

Upgrade from flimsy tools to pretty good tools.

ONE GOAL (Page 43)

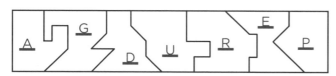

Every player's goal is to: UPGRADE.

DEAL OR DUD? (Page 44)

COLOR BY NUMBER (Page 45)

ORCHARD EXPANSION (Page 46)

TRAVELER'S REWARD (Page 47)

FIND COCONUTS ON MYSTERY ISLAND TOURS

BUG OUT (Page 48)

BUG OUT (continued)

You want the ladybug.

CROSSWORD: MILEAGE EARNER

The achievement is called CLAM AND COLLECTED. Dig up manila clams and get rewarded.

MISSING INGREDIENT (Page 51)

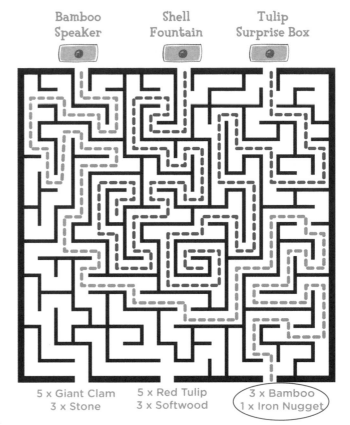

You can make the Bamboo Speaker.

GONE FISHIN' (Page 50)

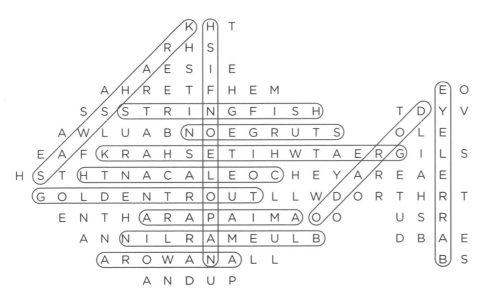

These are the most valuable fish. They're all worth ten thousand bells and up.

GROWING GOALS (Page 52)

YOU CAN PLANT COCONUT
TREES ON SAND PATHS
(not just on the beach)
So start terraforming!

CONSTRUCT A WORD (Page 53)

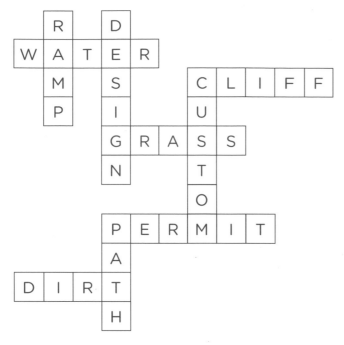

The word you constructed:
TERRAFORMING

THE ULTIMATE ANSWER (Page 54)

XDRXDR

Which translates into YES, YES

Really, isn't Tom Nook's catchphrase
the Ultimate Answer?

PERSONALITY PLUS (Page 55)

NAME	PERSONALITY	CATCHPHRASE
Eunice	Normal	Lambchop
Bree	Snooty	Cheeseball
Gabi	Peppy	Honeybun
Klaus	Smug	Strudel
Cobb	Jock	Hot Dog

Did you notice? All their catchphrases
are foods. What would your food
catchphrase be?